WATCHMAN NEE

Christ Becoming Our Wisdom

Living Stream Ministry
Anaheim, California

© 1993 Living Stream Ministry

All rights reserved. No part of this work may be reproduced or transmitted in any form or by any means—graphic, electronic, or mechanical, including photocopying, recording, or information storage and retrieval systems—without written permission from the publisher.

ISBN 1-57593-878-2

Living Stream Ministry
1853 W. Ball Road, Anaheim, CA 92804 USA
P. O. Box 2121, Anaheim, CA 92814 USA

97 98 99 00 01 \ 9 8 7 6 5 4 3 2 1

CHRIST BECOMING OUR WISDOM

Scripture Reading: 1 Cor. 1:30

The Bible speaks of Christ as our life in many ways. But the meaning of the words "Christ is our life" is not that simple. First Corinthians 1:30 explains what Christ as our life means. This passage can be divided into two sections. The first section says, "But of Him you are in Christ Jesus." This speaks of our relationship with Christ. The second section says, "Who became wisdom to us from God." This speaks of Christ's relationship with us. Putting it another way, this verse speaks of how we are in Christ and also how Christ is in us. We must pay attention to these two things. Some Christians emphasize only the first of these two aspects, while others emphasize only the second aspect. Whether one emphasizes the first aspect or the second, any bias will result in problems and sickness to our Christian life. We must have a proper knowledge of both aspects. We must know how we can be in Christ and how Christ can be in us.

God has given us the Lord Jesus. His purpose is not for Him to be our teacher or a pattern that we follow, but for us to take Him as our life, so that His life can be manifested through us. If we do not have the life of Christ, we cannot be a Christian. If we have the life of Christ but do not know how this life has become our life, we cannot be a proper Christian and readily manifest His life. How then can we have Christ as our life? This is a very basic question. The Lord Jesus is God, and He is also a man. How can we have Him as our life? This seems to be impossible. We can never solve this problem. Only God can solve this problem. God is able to do what man cannot do. First Corinthians 1:30 tells us that this work has been accomplished by God alone. If God had not done this work, it would have been impossible for Christ to become our life. The first part of this verse says, "But of Him you are in Christ Jesus." The first part of the work was done by God. The second part says, "Who became wisdom to us from God." The second part of the work was also done by God. We cannot make the Lord Jesus our wisdom; He "became wisdom to us from God." Hence, Christ as our life is something that God Himself has done. Whether it is the first or the second part, nothing is possible apart from God, and nothing will be accomplished apart from God. God has made Christ our life.

IT BEING OF GOD
THAT WE ARE IN CHRIST JESUS

God wants Christ to be our life. But how did He begin to do this? God did not first put Christ's life into us. Rather, He first put us into Christ. God first put us into Christ, and then put Christ into us. The first thing that God wants to do is build up our relationship with Christ. If we do not have a relationship with Christ, we cannot have Christ come into us to be our life. First we are in Christ, and then Christ can be in us. This is God's order of work.

Why did God put us in Christ? He put us there because we are sinful; we have the Adamic life within us. We are sinful and have the Adamic life in us; therefore, we must first be dealt with, before God can give us a new life. God cannot carry out this dealing in us directly. If He carried it out in us directly, we would die; we would not be able to live. If God dealt with our sins directly, there could be no other way and no other result than eternal death.

On the one hand, God wants to deal with our sins and our Adamic life. On the other hand, He does not wish to see us die. What then did He do? He put us in Christ by the operation of the might of His power. As a result, whatever He has done to Christ becomes His dealing with us. We are all included in Christ. Whatever God has done in Christ becomes His work in us. When God dealt with Christ, the result was the same as if He had dealt with us. This is the basic biblical truth concerning the Lord Jesus being our Savior.

God told Adam in the garden of Eden that when he disobeyed God's commandment and ate the fruit of the tree of the knowledge of good and evil, he would receive a judgment from God. What was the judgment? God declared to Adam, "For in the day that thou eatest thereof thou shalt surely die" (Gen. 2:17). It is a sin to eat the fruit forbidden by God, and the day that one sins, he will die. Death is the punishment for sin. If a man sins, he will suffer punishment. "For in the day that thou eatest thereof thou shalt surely die." This means that those who sin will surely die. If a man sins, he will surely die. It is better for man not to sin. Once he sins, death will be the sure result. Sin is a fact which cannot be overturned, and death is the inevitable result of sin; it is also something which cannot be overturned. What then should be done? On the one hand, God has to put us to death completely. On the other hand, He must cause us to live. This is the only way to salvation. Thank the Lord that He has established a salvation for us. This salvation involves sending a Savior to die on our behalf. This is why Christ had to be born. If Christ had not been born, He could not have died for us. Without the flesh, there could not have been the vicarious death. Christ became flesh, and therefore, He could die for us. Through His death, He bore our punishment and became our salvation. How could Christ die for us? He could die for us because God put us into Christ. God put us all into Christ; this is the most crucial teaching in the whole Bible. We cannot fathom and do not understand how

God exercised His power and authority to put us into Christ. All we know is that 1 Corinthians 1:30 tells us clearly that "of Him you are in Christ Jesus." "Of Him [God]" means that this is something that God has done.

What does it mean for us to be in Christ? I will explain this with an illustration. Peking produces a certain kind of lacquer box with a number of boxes being in a set. Each box in the set fits into another one. Outwardly there is only one box. But when one opens up the box, there are more boxes inside that one box; within the big box are the smaller boxes. This is the way we are in Christ. Our being in Christ is in contrast to Christ being in us. We are all descendants of Adam, and we were all in Adam. Adam is like the big box, while we were like the small boxes. The many small boxes come out of that one big box. Out of the one Adam, we were produced. When one is opened, there are many. We are the many. When we put the many into the one, we see only the one. From our side, there are many individuals. We are the many individuals. From God's side, we are only one man in Adam. This is like the many small boxes contained in the one big box. Outwardly there is only one box. Because we are all in Adam, "the disobedience of one man" constituted many sinners. Because we are all one in Adam, every one of us is condemned. God saved us according to the same principle. He has put us all into Christ, and "through the obedience of the One the many will be constituted righteous." Because we are one in Christ, we have all received justification of life (Rom. 5:18-19). God considers all of us as one person in Adam. In the same way, He considers all of us as one person in Christ. Adam is like one big box, while Christ is like a second big box. God has taken us out of the first big box and put us into the second big box. We are one in the first big box—Adam, and we are one in the second big box—Christ. The Bible calls the Lord Jesus "the second man" and "the last Adam" (1 Cor. 15:47, 45). The Lord Jesus is the last Adam, and God has included all of us in Him.

When Jesus of Nazareth was living as a man on earth, He was the unique One. But when He went to the cross, God included us all in Him. Therefore, when Jesus of Nazareth was crucified, that cross was not only His cross, but our cross as well. Because God put us into Christ, the cross is no longer just His cross, but a cross in which all those who are in Him have a part. We must realize that the cross of Christ is also our cross. If God had not put us into Christ, we would have nothing to do with the cross. Since God put us into Christ, we have a great deal to do with the cross. Thank and praise God that when Christ was crucified, we were included in Him. Since we are included in Him, His experience on the cross becomes our experience. This is what Romans 6:6 means when it says, "Our old man has been crucified with Him."

If we are not in Christ, we cannot be crucified together with Christ. Consequently, someone has said, "If we are not *in* Christ, we cannot be *with* Christ." This is a spiritual word as well as a scriptural word. We must remember that in order for us to be with Him, we have to be in Him. If we are not in Him first, we cannot be with Him. This is our fundamental faith, and we must be clear about it.

"But of Him you are in Christ Jesus." This is absolutely something that God has done. Yet we did not know this. In order for us to know, there was the need for the church to preach the gospel. The church announces to men this earth-shaking fact, that God has put men into Christ; when the Lord Jesus was crucified on the cross, God judged Him, and men were also judged in Him. Therefore, judgment is over as far as men are concerned. This is the gospel. The gospel tells us that God has done something in Christ. It tells us that God has included us in Christ. When He dealt with Christ, He also dealt with us. We have been dealt with in Him already. God has solved the problem of sin as well as the problem of ourselves. Thank the Lord that we died in Christ. This is why Romans 6:11 says, "So also you, reckon yourselves to be dead to sin, but living to God in Christ Jesus."

We are dead in Christ Jesus. What do we do after we hear such a fact? We are persons with a will. After we believe in this fact, we should have some kind of expression. Therefore, we want to be baptized after we believe in the Lord and are saved. What is the meaning of baptism? Being baptized is being in Christ Jesus and being in His death (Rom. 6:3-4). In other words, God has put us into Christ, but we have to do something to show others that we are in Christ. Our baptism demonstrates to others the way we get into Christ. When we are baptized into the water, do we remain in the water? No, we come out of it quickly. Our coming out of the water signifies that we have been resurrected with Christ. Whoever comes out of the water testifies that he has resurrected. Hence, our baptism is a reenactment of the work that God accomplished for us in Christ. It is a performance to show others what God did for us in Christ. This is a spiritual performance.

When Christ was on the cross, God put us in Christ and terminated the old man in Adam. God had to terminate Adam; that account had to be settled and closed. We were men in Adam, and we could only be delivered from Adam through death. When we are joined to the death of Christ, we are terminated and delivered from Adam. This is the first aspect of God's work. The second aspect of God's work is to put Christ into us. First Corinthians 1:30 says, "Who became wisdom to us from God."

"WHO BECAME ... FROM GOD"

We have spoken of our being in Christ. Now we will speak on Christ being in us.

How can Christ be in us? Christ is in us because of resurrection. Because the Lord Jesus has resurrected and because He is now in the Holy Spirit (He is not merely a man, but a man in the Spirit), He can be in us. The Lord said that His flesh is meat indeed and His blood is drink indeed. He can be eaten by us (John 6:53-56). If He were still a man like He was when He was on earth, He could not be eaten by us. We eat the fruit of the tree of life; we do not eat the tree of life itself. We cannot eat the tree; there is no way we can take the tree into us. When the Lord Jesus was on earth, He was like the tree of life; there was no way for us to take Him into us. In the same way, there is no way for us to take a person into us today. If the Lord Jesus were not a resurrected Lord, if He were only a Lord who once lived on the earth, He could only be Himself forever, while I could only be myself forever. There would be no way for us to receive Him. It would not matter how holy and lovely Jesus of Nazareth was; there would be no way for us to receive Him, because He would only be a man. But thank the Lord that He is not only a man today; He has died and resurrected. In the Holy Spirit,

He has become the Lord whom we can receive. The Holy Spirit is the Lord's coming in another form (14:16-20). Another name for the Holy Spirit is "the Spirit of Jesus" (Acts 16:7). He is also called "the Spirit of Christ" (Rom. 8:9). When the Lord Jesus put on the Holy Spirit, He became a "receivable" Lord. If He had not become such a Lord, we would not be able to enjoy Him. Christ has resurrected and put on the Holy Spirit. When we receive the Holy Spirit, we receive Christ; in the same way, when we receive the Son, we receive the Father. When men in the past saw the Father, they saw the Son; in the same way, when men know the Spirit today, they know the Son. The Lord Jesus has resurrected, and He is in the Holy Spirit. Therefore, we can receive Him into us to be our life. All those who have received the Lord Jesus, whether they are clear or not, have received this experience from God.

God has put us into Christ. This is the first thing. The second thing is that He has made Christ our wisdom. Neither of these two things have been done by us. We cannot get into Christ by ourselves, and we cannot put Christ into us. Both things could only be accomplished by God.

Christ became wisdom to us from God. What does this mean? First I would point out the proper punctuation for the second part of 1 Corinthians 1:30. According to the original language, there should be a colon after the words "wisdom to us from God." This means that wisdom includes the following three things: righteousness, sanctification, and redemption. First Corinthians 1—3 speaks of God's wisdom and man's wisdom. Wisdom is the subject, and righteousness, sanctification, and redemption are the explanation of how Christ becomes our wisdom.

What does this verse mean? In order to understand this verse, we must first consider what life is. Suppose a temptation comes and stirs you up. You know that you have to be patient. But where does this patience come from? Your life supplies you with patience. You need to have life before you can exercise your patience. When you do not have life, you are dead, and there is no way for you to practice patience. You must supply and sustain your patience with life. Suppose you realize that laziness is wrong, and you want to be diligent. If you are diligent, your life is making you diligent. Suppose a man has encountered hardships, and you think that you should love him and help him. Where does this love come from? It is your life that compels you to love. Therefore, the inward reaction that is produced every time we encounter something is the result of the flow of life. These reactions originate from your life. The source of power for these reactions is life. Without life there can be no reaction. We only react when there is life. Every moment of our life we are dealing with things, and every moment we have reactions. We deal with the demands of the outward world moment by moment with our life. Moment by moment we are exercising our life.

God has not given us Christ so that He could just die for us on the cross; He has given Christ to us to be our life. Originally, we react to all the demands that are outside of us by exercising our own life; we act according to our own life. If our own life is strong enough, we make it. If our own life is not strong enough, we do not make it, or worse, we collapse. We react with our own life and deal with outward matters with our own life. But

God has given Christ to us to be our life. Before we received the Lord Jesus, we lived by ourselves. After we receive the Lord Jesus, God wants Him to live inside of us and live for us. When the Lord Jesus becomes our life within, we do not have to live by our original life. It is not a matter of the Lord Jesus giving us commands, suggestions, or teachings and then us carrying them out. Rather, He becomes our life within and carries things out for us. From now on, we should live by His life. Formerly, we responded to outward demands with our own life. Now we should allow Christ's life to respond to them.

After understanding the meaning of Christ being our life, we now come to the question of Christ becoming our wisdom from God. Brothers and sisters, you have been a Christian for many years. Do you have anything other than your own wisdom? Have you received the Lord Jesus as your wisdom? Has the Lord Jesus been your wisdom once? How much have you known the Lord Jesus? This is the basic question, and we must be clear about it. This verse does not say that the Lord Jesus gives us wisdom; it does not say that God has given us the Lord Jesus' wisdom. It does not say that we understand and know how to speak or act, even though we were once foolish, because God has given us wisdom. No, the Bible does not say this. The Bible says that Christ became wisdom to us from God. The word "became" is very important, and there is no better word than this word. We can take the story of Moses and Aaron as an example. Moses was afraid of speaking to the Israelites; he was afraid because he was not eloquent. He said that he was slow of speech and of a slow tongue; therefore, he dared not go. What did God say? He said, "Is not Aaron the Levite thy brother?...He shall be thy spokesman unto the people: and he shall be, even he shall be to thee instead of a mouth" (Exo. 4:14, 16). Does this mean that when Aaron became Moses' mouth, Moses became eloquent? No, Aaron only became Moses' mouth, but Moses was still Moses. (Of course, Moses spoke later. But that is a different story.) When Moses' eloquence failed, he could ask Aaron to speak for him. This is the meaning of Aaron becoming Moses' mouth. Aaron became Moses' mouth. The eloquence was still with Aaron; it was not with Moses. Moses needed Aaron to be the mouth, because his own mouth did not work as well. It does not mean that after Moses took Aaron as his mouth, his own mouth became eloquent.

After we see the meaning of Aaron becoming the mouth of Moses, we see the meaning of Christ becoming wisdom to us from God. It does not mean that Christ has made us wise. Rather, it means that we are foolish, but we allow the Lord to become our wisdom while we do not move. Originally, when there were demands from the outside, we reacted with our own life. Today when there are demands from the outside, we know that we cannot make it and should not react anymore. What then should we do? We should allow the Lord's life to react. It is not a matter of becoming better in ourselves; it is a matter of the Lord living on our behalf. Moses' mouth did not improve. Rather, Aaron became his mouth for him and spoke instead of him. Christ being our wisdom is like Aaron speaking on Moses' behalf. Suppose you are going to speak to someone. What are you going to do when you cannot say what you want to say? You may ask another one who has come with you to speak for you. You cannot speak yourself, and you ask him to speak; he meets the demand. While he is speaking, your mouth remains dumb; it has not improved, and you are still the same as before. We must never think that when Christ becomes our wisdom, we become wise. We must remember that even when Christ has become our wisdom, we can still do nothing in ourselves.

Galatians 2:20 says, "It is no longer I who live, but it is Christ who lives in me." This is a fact. This shows us how a Christian should live. He should live by not doing anything by himself, but by allowing Christ to do everything. In other words, let Aaron speak and Moses be quiet. Some people are not eloquent, yet they need to speak. What do they do? They ask you to speak for them. But while you are speaking, they are not satisfied; they interrupt with a word or two. This makes it very difficult for you. If Moses' mouth could not speak, he should take Aaron's mouth as his mouth. Thank the Lord that this is God's way of salvation. God did not change Moses' mouth; rather, He gave him a new mouth. God does not change a person's mouth; He gives him another mouth. God does not change a foolish man into a wise man; rather, He causes Christ to become wisdom to the foolish man. Brothers and sisters, this is salvation. God has not changed foolish men into wise; rather, He has made Christ our wisdom; Christ has become wisdom to us from God.

Suppose a matter needs great wisdom to handle and settle it. You may try this way and that way in vain; your little mind may be exhausted, yet you still cannot come up with a solution. Then you say, "Lord, I am foolish. If it is left up to me to do, I will surely not be able to make it. I can only look to You. You do it for me." After you have trusted in the Lord this way, the Lord may direct you to do something, say something, or take some action, and you may not even be aware of the great wisdom involved in doing these things. But after you have done them, one day you will say, "What I did that day was not something that I could have done by myself. What I said that day was not something that I could have said by myself." This means that you have not changed at all; it was the Lord who became your wisdom. This is Christ becoming wisdom to you. Originally, we had to handle things by ourselves, yet we could not handle them. So we allowed Christ to be our wisdom. We have to remember that Christ's wisdom does not become our wisdom. In addition, Christ is not giving us wisdom so that we can become wise. Instead, Christ in us is becoming wisdom to us. Wisdom belongs to the Lord and not to us. He is our wisdom; He is becoming our wisdom. Brothers and sisters, if we know what it means for Christ to "become," we can live a proper life before the Lord.

We have previously said that Christ becoming our wisdom means three things: righteousness, sanctification, and redemption. What do these things mean? Let us first consider righteousness. Then we will speak on the other two.

Christ Becoming Our Righteousness

We need righteousness before God. Righteousness has a great deal to do with God. If we did not have to stand before God, the question of righteousness would not come in. Once we think about God, we think of righteousness. For example, when we have to meet people, we always think of our dress. In the same way, when a man meets God, he must have righteousness. Without righteousness, no one can see God. Hence, righteousness is a basic item in the Christian life. The matter of righteousness involves the means by which we come to God every time we approach Him. If a Christian has not settled this matter, he does not have a solid foundation. A Christian who has doubts about righteousness cannot come to God with assurance. Many Christians desire to grow, and they would like to go on in God's way. But one of the reasons they go back and forth is that they are not clear about righteousness. Righteousness is a simple matter, yet it is foundational. Brothers and sisters, if we are not clear about righteousness, we cannot go on in peace; we will always have trouble. Hence, we must be clear about the matter of righteousness.

We are often not sure by what means we can come to God. We think that our good behavior is our righteousness and that we come to God by good behavior. Some brothers and sisters think that if their behavior is good and they do well from morning to evening, they have righteousness that day. But if their behavior is not perfect, they have a problem with righteousness. The brothers and sisters who have this kind of thought take righteousness as their conduct.

When God opens our eyes, we will see that our righteousness before God has nothing to do with our conduct; it is something else. God's light is like a knife to us; it divides our righteousness from our conduct. Formerly, we thought that when we came to God, our conduct was our righteousness. But now we see that when we come to God, Christ is our righteousness. Our righteousness is no longer our conduct; our righteousness is Christ. Thank the Lord that before God, our righteousness is Christ. Our conduct can improve, but our righteousness cannot improve. Our conduct is not perfect, but our righteousness is always perfect. Our righteousness is Christ, and we can come to God through Christ. Our conduct is not blameless, but praise the Lord, our righteousness is blameless because our righteousness is Christ.

We have to know that Christ as our righteousness is the greatest salvation. God has settled the matter of righteousness for us, and our position before God is secured. Brothers and sisters, we should have good behavior, and we should behave well. We should serve God more, and we should be diligent and bear the cross. But we have to realize that while our conduct can improve again and again, our righteousness before God cannot improve anymore. The means by which we can come to God today is the same means by which we can come to Him ten or twenty years from now. Our righteousness before God is not our own conduct; it is Christ. If a man does not have the revelation to see that Christ is his righteousness, he will not be able to come boldly before God. If he sees that his righteousness is a person, that his righteousness is Christ, he will be bold in approaching God. Brothers and sisters, we must remember that when we come to God, our righteousness is not our conduct. Our righteousness is not a thing; our righteousness is a person—Christ.

Christ Becoming Our Sanctification

Before God, our righteousness is not our conduct. But this does not mean that we do not have to care for our conduct while we live on earth. Our righteousness before God is settled, but what should we do about our conduct and living? We must see that God has made Christ not only our righteousness, but our sanctification as well. This sanctification is not a thing or condition, but a person—Christ. God has made Christ our sanctification.

Some Christians have a certain concept about sanctification. They think that sanctification is Christ helping them to be sanctified. This means that they are not holy, but they will become holy through Christ's help. First Corinthians 1:30 tells us that God has made Christ sanctification to us. We do not have to try to be sanctified by ourselves. We do not become sanctified through the help of Christ. Christ Himself has become our sanctification. Our sanctification is the person of Christ, not the help of Christ.

Some Christians think that sanctification is Christ empowering them to become holy. They pray for the Lord to give them strength. They think that as long as they have the strength, they can be sanctified. But God's Word does not say that we can be sanctified. It does not say that Christ gives us the strength to be holy. God's Word tells us clearly that He has made Christ sanctification to us. Our sanctification is a gift. Our sanctification is a person. Our sanctification is not the result of a power from God. If we do not have the vision, we will not see the vast difference between these two things. This is not something that our mind can comprehend. If we do not have the revelation, it is useless even if our mind understands. God must show us that Christ does not come to help us to become holy; He does not give us the strength to be sanctified. Rather, He Himself is our sanctification.

Many Christians believe that there are two things related to sanctification. One is the power of sanctification, and the other is the fruit of sanctification. They think that a man must have the power of sanctification before he can bear the fruit of sanctification. According to this theory, where should we put Christ? Should Christ be on the side of power, which means that Christ as our power enables us to become sanctified? Yet God's speaking in 1 Corinthians 1:30 is totally different from this theory. Christ did not come to be our power of sanctification. Christ Himself is our sanctification. He did not come to be our power of sanctification to enable us to produce sanctification. He Himself is sanctification. I have to shout Hallelujah! He does not become our power of sanctification, which enables us to produce sanctification. Rather, we have Christ; therefore, we have sanctification. Brothers and sisters, if we say that sanctification is a thing, God's Word will tell us that Christ is that thing. Brothers and sisters, our thing is a living person. Our sanctification is a living person. Our thing is Christ; our sanctification is Christ.

We can take humility as an example. Suppose I am a very proud person. I am aware of my pride, yet I cannot humble myself. Therefore, I pray, "God, be merciful to me. Please send the Lord Jesus to help me so that I can be humble." Brothers and sisters, have you seen this? I have made Christ my help in trying to be humble. I think that with His help I can become humble. Therefore, I ask Christ to help me to become humble. But this is my concept; this is not God's way of salvation. God does not ask Christ to help me to become humble. God gives me Christ, who is my humility. God has not given us Christ as a power so that we can produce humility; God has given us Christ to be our humility. Brothers and sisters, does the Lord have power? Yes, every one of us knows that He has power. Has He given us this power? Yes, He has given us this power. Then why are we still so weak? We have to realize that He has given all the power to us already, but we cannot use this power. The Lord's power is real, but we cannot use it. If we try to be humble by the Lord's power, we find that we cannot make it. At the most we perform some outward acts which we call humility. But inwardly, there is no such thing as humility. God's Word shows us that our humility is not the power of Christ, but Christ Himself.

What does it mean for us to say that humility is just the Lord Himself? It means that I do not have any humility and I cannot be humble. Even if the Lord gives me the strength to humble myself, I still cannot be humble. I can only say to the Lord, "You are my humility. I allow You to become my humility." Brothers and sisters, what is the meaning of Christ becoming my humility? Simply put, it means that Christ replaces me and expresses His own humility in my place. When we ask God for power to humble ourselves, we may be able to humble ourselves for a while, but this humility is merely good behavior, a good attitude, a good intention, and a good condition. This humility is not Christ. When we ask the Lord to be our humility, we lift up our heads and say to Him, "Lord, I do not have any humility in me. Even if You give me the strength to humble myself, I still would not have humility. Therefore Lord, I ask that You come and be my humility and that You be humble in my place." After we look to the Lord this way, any humility that we begin to have will be a spontaneous humility. Such humility will not be a work, but a living person—Christ Himself.

Take patience as an example. I do not have any patience, and I cannot be patient. My patience is just Christ Himself. The same is true with meekness. I do not have any meekness, and I cannot be meek. My meekness is just Christ Himself. Brothers and sisters, have you seen this? God has made Christ my patience. God has made Christ my meekness. All our virtues are just Christ. Christian virtues are different from common human virtues. The virtues that we commonly speak of are individual things, but Christian virtues are not individual, fragmentary things, but a living person, who is Christ Himself. Our virtue is not plural in number, but singular in number. Our virtue is not fragmentary things, but a person. Brothers and sisters, if we do not have Christ, we do not have anything.

When Christ becomes our life within, He responds to all the demands outside of us. There is only one life, but because the demands outside of us are different, there are different kinds of responses. When pride comes, Christ is manifested as our humility. When anxiety comes, Christ is manifested as our patience. When jealousy comes, Christ is manifested as our love. From this one life issue all the virtues. Because the need in the environment varies, the manifestations of this life also vary. Daily we encounter many things. When the Lord manifests Himself in these things, we find Him in many virtues. Hence, the many virtues of Christians are not their own behavior, but the reflections of Christ and the manifestations of Christ. This is the meaning of Christ becoming our sanctification.

Hence, the Christian life is a matter of how much we know about Christ. It is not a matter of our humility, our patience, or our meekness. Everything depends on

Christ. The more we know Christ, the more His virtues are manifested through us. Others may think that these are our virtues. But we know that they are nothing but Christ. A Christian has no virtue other than Christ. All Christian virtues are just Christ. Brothers and sisters, if we know Christ more, we will see that our virtues are just the outflow of Christ. Sister Wang's patience is Christ. Brother Chan's patience is also Christ. Brother Chow's love, Sister Hu's meekness, and Sister Liu's humility are not different virtues; they are Christ. The virtues manifested through different persons are different. But they are all Christ. Hallelujah! All of our virtues are just Christ! Everything that flows out of us is just Christ. The love that flows out of Brother Chow is Christ. The meekness that flows out of Sister Hu is Christ. The humility that flows out of Sister Liu is also Christ. The demands in the environment may be different, but the supply within is the same. The outward manifestations are different, but the intrinsic nature is the same. No Christian virtue is a product of one's own work; every virtue is the outflow of Christ. It is Christ reflecting Himself out of us.

Brothers and sisters, once we realize this, we will lift up our head to the Lord and say, "I have tried in the past to be a Christian by myself. I was wrong. Lord, I thank You. Now I know that You are my sanctification. I want You to live Yourself out of me."

Christ Becoming Our Redemption

Not only has Christ become righteousness to us from God, and not only has He become sanctification to us from God, but He has become redemption to us from God. The meaning of redemption is to buy back or to free by paying a ransom. There are three things which are indispensable in any act of redemption. The first is the person redeemed, the second is the redeemer, and the third is the price of redemption. All the redeemed ones were formerly sold under sin (Rom. 7:14); they were the slaves of sin. Now the Lord Jesus has paid the price of the blood (Matt. 20:28; Mark 10:45; 1 Tim. 2:6) and has redeemed us out of the curse of the law (Gal. 3:13). This shows us that the Lord is our Redeemer.

But we have to go on one step further. The Lord Jesus is not only our Redeemer, but also our redemption. If the Lord Jesus is only our Redeemer, He is still separated from the redeemed ones, in spite of the close relationship between the two—a relationship of grace, of saving our lives. The Lord Jesus has not only become our Redeemer but has become our redemption. This means that when we are redeemed, we are not only joined to a thing, but to a person. When we are redeemed, the Lord Jesus becomes one with us; the two become one. Our redemption is a person. When we have Him, we have redemption. Without Him we do not have redemption. If we want redemption, we need Him. Once we have Him, we have redemption because He is the redemption. Our redemption is not just a thing. Our redemption is a person who is joined to us.

Christ has become our redemption. Therefore, all those who have been washed by the blood can come boldly to God. While God judges the sinners, He can righteously pass over all those who are under the blood of the Lamb (Exo. 12:12-13; Rom. 3:25-26). All the redeemed ones have experienced a full redemption. In God's eyes, all He sees is Christ. It is as if He does not see any person; all He sees is Christ. Christ is the slain Lamb; His blood removes man's sin-record before God. When a man comes to God through Christ, God will no longer condemn him, because Christ has satisfied God's righteous requirement on man's behalf. He has borne sin's punishment on man's behalf. Once a man has Christ, he has redemption. When God sees Christ, He sees redemption.

Christ is not only our redemption before God; He is also redemption within us. Christ as our redemption within is particularly related to our body. Christ as our redemption within not only delivers us from the law of sin in our members (Rom. 7:23; 8:2), but has become life to our body. Romans 8:11 says, "And if the Spirit of the One who raised Jesus from the dead dwells in you, He who raised Christ Jesus from the dead will also give life to your mortal bodies through His Spirit who indwells you." This does not mean that we will be resurrected after we die. It means that He will give life to our mortal bodies today. Second Corinthians 4:10-11 says, "Always bearing about in the body the putting to death of Jesus that the life of Jesus also may be manifested in our body. For we who are alive are always being delivered unto death for Jesus' sake that the life of Jesus also may be manifested in our mortal flesh." The most outstanding thing here is that verse 11 seems to be a repetition of verse 10. Actually it is not a repetition. Verse 10 says that the life of Jesus is manifested in our *body,* while verse 11 says that the life of Jesus is manifested in our mortal bodies. With many believers, the life of Jesus may be manifested in their body, but may not be manifested in their mortal body. The difference here is great. Many believers are obedient and patient in times of sickness; they are not anxious, and they do not murmur. They feel the Lord's presence and manifest the Lord's virtues in their expression, their voice, and their actions. Indeed the life of Jesus is manifested in their body through the Holy Spirit. Yet they do not know that the Lord Jesus is able to heal their sickness. They do not know that the Lord Jesus' life is also for their body of humiliation. They receive grace from the Lord to endure the pain, but they do not receive the healing. They have the experience of verse 10, but do not have the experience of verse 11. Brothers and sisters, we have to realize that Christ is redemption to our body. For our mortal body to be made alive does not mean that the nature of the body is changed or that we become immortal. The nature of the body remains the same, but a new life comes in to supply strength to the body. Originally, the natural life was the source of strength of our body. Now we are supplied by the life of Christ. When our body is sustained by the resurrection life of Christ, our body is enabled to work in a strong way.

Christ becoming our redemption is a big subject. Christ as our redemption is not merely a matter of Him being the life of our body today, but it affords us a great hope, which is "the redemption of our body" (Rom. 8:21-23; 1 Cor. 15:50-54; Phil. 3:21). One day God will show everyone the way that He has redeemed the creation and the way that He made us His own. Then our body will be redeemed and will put off corruption to put on incorruption; we will no longer be under the bondage of corruption, and we will enter into the liberty of glory. Then the dead will rise up, and we will be changed. Our body of humiliation will be transfigured to be conformed to the body of His glory. Then we will see that our redemption is Christ! Who are those who have the assurance that they will be in the first (the best) resurrection? Who are those who have the assurance that their body will be transfigured one day? We believe and we have the assurance because Christ is our redemption.

First Corinthians 15:42-44 shows us that when a Christian dies, he is not buried, but is "sown." We know that to sow something and to bury something are two entirely different things. For example, when you bury a piece of copper in the ground, that is all there is to it; it will not grow up again. But if you sow a grain of wheat into the ground, it will grow after a few days. When a Christian dies, he is not like a piece of copper buried in the ground, but like a grain of wheat sown into the earth. One day he will spring up again. He can spring up again because he has the life of Christ within him. This life is a life that cannot be imprisoned by death, because the life of Christ is the resurrection life. This life is in the believer. This is why he will resurrect one day. Because Christ is our redemption, He will make us grow. Christ will not be imprisoned by death. A regenerated Christian has Christ within him. Christ is his redemption, and he will inherit a resurrected body which is incorruptible, glorious, strong, and spiritual.

This is not all. Because Christ is our redemption, some Christians will not see death, but will be raptured. There was a young girl who once asked a preacher, "Does it not take a great effort for a Christian to be raptured away?" For a child, the rapture takes great effort. But we know that the rapture is not something according to our concept. A Christian is raptured because Christ is in him. Christ is his redemption, and Christ will take him away.

Christ as our life is the foundation of the Christian life. The first step in our salvation is regeneration. The last step in our salvation is the redemption of our body. But from beginning to end, the basis is Christ as our life. The relationship between Christ and us is a life relationship. In other words, it is an indissoluble relationship. Christ does not become something outside of us. He has come into us to be our life. A relationship in life is an indissoluble relationship. If we have not received Christ as our life, we have nothing to do with Christ. But since we have received Christ as our life, we have an indissoluble relationship with Him. After Adam sinned, God immediately guarded the way of the tree of life with the cherubim and a flaming sword which turned every way (Gen. 3:24). He did this because if Adam had eaten the fruit of the tree of life, he would have bonded an indissoluble relationship with God. Thank God that our relationship with Christ is a relationship which Adam did not have; it is an indissoluble relationship. Even God Himself cannot dissolve this relationship. This life lives in us all the time, and it is bringing us into glory, into eternity. What a great power this is! What a glorious hope this is!

May the Lord open our eyes to see that God has put us into Christ and made Christ our wisdom: righteousness, sanctification, and redemption. May the Lord show us that of all the gifts He has given us, none is greater than His Son. May the Lord show us that Christ is the gift and also all the gifts. He is the singular gift and also the plural gifts. We have to learn to know Christ as our wisdom. We have to learn to know Christ as our righteousness, we have to learn to know Christ as our sanctification, and we have to learn to know Christ as our redemption. May the Lord deliver us from foolishness and darkness so that we realize that there is no matter or thing in the spiritual realm. All we have is just Christ.